Welcome to
ENGLAND

Text by Margaret Friskey
Sketches by Lois Axeman

CHILDRENS PRESS, CHICAGO

Welcome to the World Books
Created by T. A. Chacharon & Associates, Ltd.

Library of Congress Cataloging in Publication Data
Friskey, Margaret.
  Welcome to England.
  (Welcome to the world)
  SUMMARY: Briefly introduces some of England's
  more popular tourist attractions of particular interest
  to children.
1. England—Description and travel—1971-
—Guide-books—Juvenile literature. [1. England—
Description and travel] I. Axeman, Lois, illus.
II. Title.
DA650.F74   914.2'04'85   74-11172
ISBN 0-516-03707-2

Photographs courtesy of British Tourist Authority.

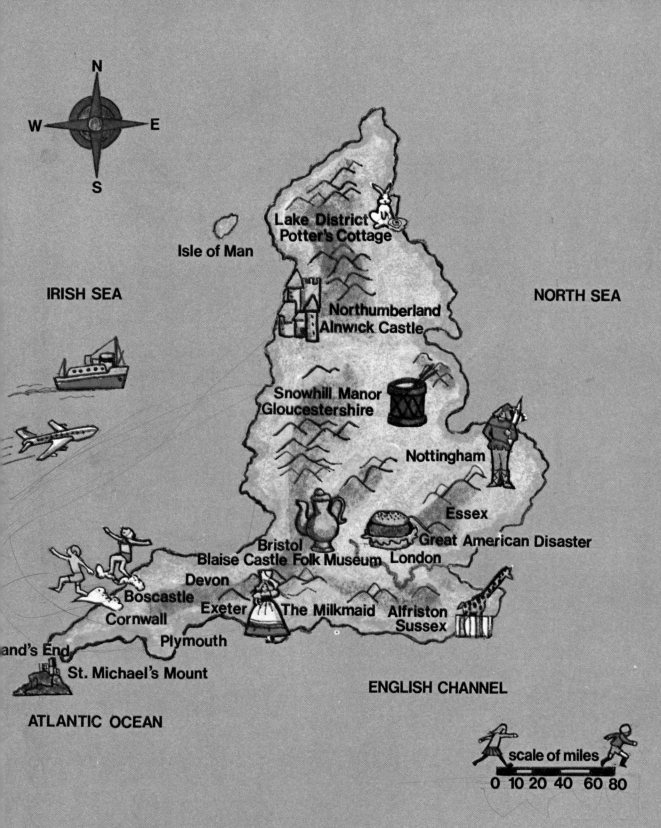

N

W   E

S

Lake District
Potter's Cottage

Isle of Man

IRISH SEA

NORTH SEA

Northumberland
Alnwick Castle

Snowhill Manor
Gloucestershire

Nottingham

Essex

Bristol
Blaise Castle Folk Museum

Great American Disaster
London

Devon

Boscastle

Cornwall

Exeter   The Milkmaid   Alfriston
Sussex

Plymouth

and's End

St. Michael's Mount

ENGLISH CHANNEL

ATLANTIC OCEAN

scale of miles
0 10 20 40 60 80

Welcome to London, the capital city. It is enormous. It is old and it is modern. It is fascinating.

Street names in London invite you to walk.

There is Petticoat Lane and Threadneedle Street, for instance.

And here is Piccadilly Circus.

It is a busy spot ringed by shops and humming with traffic.

From Piccadilly Circus you can walk down Haymarket. Turn left at the end of this busy street.

You will be in Trafalgar Square.

London, big as it is, is full of breathing spaces. This one is in the heart of the city.

Office workers come out here to sit in the sun at lunchtime. Children play in the fountains and feed the pigeons.

The statue of Lord Nelson,
hero of the battle of Trafalgar,
towers above the square.

The famous red sight-seeing
buses line up in front of the
National Gallery.

Take one of them to the nine-
hundred-year-old Tower of London.
This was a grim prison in the days
when the monarch had the power of
life and death over all the people.

Now the monarch serves England under the laws made by Parliament.

Buckingham Palace has been the London home of the royal family ever since the days of Queen Victoria.

Any day, you can see the colorful changing of the guards at the palace.

On special days, like the Queen's birthday, or the opening of Parliament, you can see Trooping the Colors. This is a most spectacular sight.

If you love books go to see
the home of Charles Dickens on
Doughty Street. You will find it
much as it was when he wrote *Oliver
Twist* and *David Copperfield.*

The Science Museum is also worth
a visit. Here is the Rolls Royce
Silver Ghost, and *Puffing Billy*,
the oldest steam engine.

There are many push-button models
you can operate.

The friendly policemen in
London are called *Bobbies*.
They do not carry guns.
If one of them meets an
American visitor he may stop
and say,
"Be careful crossing streets.
Remember that all traffic here
runs on the left instead of
on the right as it does in
your country."

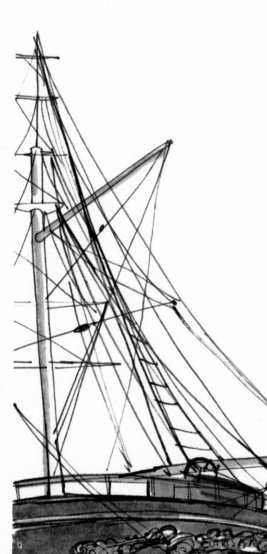

London is not on the sea.

But it is connected with it by the Thames (say Temz) River that runs through the city.

Walk along the Embankment and watch the endless activity on the river.

A short boat ride down the river will take you to the Greenwich Pier. You can see the *Cutty Sark*. It is the last of the great tea clippers.

When you want to stop and rest, enjoy one of the beautiful parks. London has more of them than any capital city.

London even has a forest at its doorstep. Six thousand acres of it stretch from London's Forest Gate to Epping. It is a real forest with old trees, deer, lakes, and a royal hunting lodge.

Regent's Park in the city is a sea of tulips in the spring. This whole great area was once the fenced-in hunting park of Henry VIII.

As a change of pace, ride through the park to the zoo in a canal boat.

A mews is a group of stables around an open space or alley.

At the Royal Mews, Buckingham Palace Road, you can see the Queen's horses and the coaches used on state occasions.

People whose address is a mews may be living in homes that were once thick-walled stables.

Lennox Gardens Mews is one of the fashionable places to live in London.

You could linger for weeks in the city of London. But there is more of England to see.

Distances are never great in this small country. And there are many ways to travel.

You can ride a car, a motor coach, a plane, a train, or even a boat.

There are almost three thousand miles of rivers and canals in England.

Visit an old castle.

This one is high on an island called Saint Michael's Mount.

It is near the southwest tip of England called Land's End.

King Arthur's Court is said to have met near here.

Climb through the village to the castle. You will hear stories of pirates and rebels and giants.

You may hear about the two skeletons found in a wall.

Thousands of years ago, each lord of a castle was like a king. He had his own army of knights.

Farmers built their homes near the castle for protection.

Bodiam Castle is in southern England, too. It has a moat around it for protection. Now the moat is filled with water lilies.

There are castles all over England that you can visit.

About three hundred years before
Columbus discovered America, England
was united under one king.

Private armies were outlawed. But
it took many years to get rid of
all of them.

England is proud of its history
and keeps it alive.

Sometimes children act out an
attack on a castle or manor house.

England is a small country.

You are never far from water. The North Sea is on the east. The English Channel is on the south. The Irish Sea and the Atlantic Ocean are on the west.

The sea always has played an important part in the lives of the people.

There are rocky cliffs, inlets, beaches and harbors.

Plymouth is a naval base. Sir Francis Drake lived near here.

The Pilgrims waited here to sail to the New World.

Walk down the narrow streets
of this quaint village near
Plymouth.

The stone houses seem to have
grown from the ground. And in a
way they did. They were built
with the materials at hand.

They are snug and timeless
under their thatched roofs.

Thanks to the Gulf Stream in the Atlantic Ocean, the climate is mild in this southwest tip of England. It is a resort area with many beautiful beaches.

Many village streets, like those in Boscastle, lead to water. There are many pleasure boats and fishing boats. There are men working to make a living from the sea.

Go south from London into
Sussex. Walk up the cobbled
street in the village of Rye.

You will come to the Mermaid
Inn with its fine half-timbering.

This old inn was used by
smugglers for hundreds of years.

Queen Elizabeth stayed here
in 1573. You can stay here, too,
if you like.

Staying at old village inns
is a very pleasant way to see
England.

Each village is different.
Each has its own charm. Some
have stone houses with thatched
roofs. Some are on the seacoast.

If you go north of London
into Essex, you will come to
Finchingfield. Here the neat
white houses face a mill pond.

If you want to feel like a
country squire returning to his
estate, stay at one of the old
manor houses. Some of these large
historic homes have been made
into hotels.

Many others are open to the
public, even though you cannot
stay in them. You can walk through
the spacious rooms. They are filled
with art treasures, beautiful furni-
ture, and china.

Lower Huxley Hall in Cheshire is
a typical manor house. It was
built three hundred years ago.

Scattered through the Midlands, in the center of England, there are many small farms.

Wheat, barley, oats, and potatoes are raised on this gently rolling land.

Streams, rivers, and canals cut through it.

There are dairy farms. There are sheep, cows and horses in the pastures.

Some of the best of England is in the northwest. Go through Robin Hood country at Nottingham. Stop in the Lake District.

Mountains and lakes in this National Park invite hikers.

Beatrix Potter's little cottage is here. You almost expect Peter Rabbit himself to open the door.

It is a short hop to the Isle of Man. Visit a castle, swim, and marvel at the size of the water wheel.

Surely, there is more in England than you can see in one visit.

Come again and again.

Cheerio!

Exciting places to see

Castles
Alnwick Castle, Northumberland
Bodiam Castle, Sussex
Dover Castle, Kent
Dunster Castle, Somerset
Warwick Castle, Warwickshire
Sudeley Castle, Gloucestershire
Caves
Cheddar Caves, Somerset
Wookey Hole Caves, Somerset
Miniature Railways You Can Ride On
Bluebell Railway, Sussex
Romney, Hythe, and Dymchurch, Kent
Stapleford House and Park, Leicestershire

Museums You'll Enjoy
Blaise Castle Folk Museum, Bristol. Life in an 18th-century house
National Motor Museum, Hampshire. Old cars and motorcycles
Shuttleworth Collection, Bedfordshire. Old airplanes, cars and bicycles
Open Air Museum, Sussex. Historic buildings including a medieval farmhouse and a Saxon weaver's hut
H.M.S. Victory, Portsmouth. Admiral Lord Nelson's flagship
Snowshill Manor, Gloucestershire. Musical instruments, clocks, toys
Whitby Museum, Yorkshire. Model sailing ships and whalers, mementoes of Captain Cook

Fun places to eat

In London
Charing Cross Pier, a glass-walled restaurant that floats on the Thames
Derry and Toms Roof Garden, a restaurant in a real garden with ducks in a pond
Post Office Tower, a restaurant that revolves on the top of London's tallest building
Great American Disaster, a place to go if you're homesick for real American hamburgers
In Chester
The Paddock
In Plymouth
Dartmoor Restaurant
Perila's Fish Restaurant
In Exeter
The Milkmaid
In York
Terry's Restaurant
Betty's Restaurant
In Cardiff
The Louise
David Morgan, The Hayes
And almost anywhere
Look for a fish and chip shop
For an extra special treat
Many famous castles and inns offer medieval banquets with medieval dishes, music, and costumed waitresses

Special sights in and around London

Battersea Pleasure Gardens and Fun Fair

The Changing of the Guard at Buckingham Palace and the Horseguards, Whitehall

Hampton Court Palace and Gardens. Henry VIII lived here. You'll enjoy getting "lost" in the maze of hedges

Kew Gardens. The oldest and largest collection of plants in the world

Madame Tussaud's. Wax models of famous people, including some scary villains

Natural History Museum. Animals, rocks, plants, insects. They'll let you make sketches and give you the materials

Pollock's Toy Museum and Toy Theatres

Little Angel's Marionette Theatre

Royal Mews. See the coaches and horses used by the Royal Family

The Tower of London. See the beefeaters, armor and historic uniforms, and the priceless Crown Jewels

Unicorn Theatre. Special plays for children

Science Museum. With the oldest steam engine and lots of pushbutton models

Windsor Castle. See one of the places the Royal Family lives

Zoos

Crystal Palace Children's Zoo, London
Regent's Park, London
Whipsnade, Bedfordshire
Windsor Safari Park, Berkshire
Woburn Abbey Park, Bedfordshire
Alfriston, Sussex
Chester Zoological Gardens, Cheshire
Jersey Zoo, Channel Islands
Longleat Game Reserve, Wiltshire
Norfolk Wildlife Park
Suffolk Wildlife Park

English people and Americans speak the same language. However, each uses different words for some of the same things. Here are a few examples.

ENGLISH	AMERICAN
holiday	vacation
seaside	beach
lift	elevator
petrol	gasoline
bobby/copper	policeman/cop
pillar box	mailbox
post	mail
torch	flashlight
tinned	canned
lorry	truck
tube/underground	subway
pram	baby carriage
gym shoes	sneakers
cupboard	closet
biscuits (sweet)	cookies
biscuits (water/cheese)	crackers
dustman	garbage man
serviette	napkin
flannel	washcloth
sweet	dessert
sweets	candy
roundabout	merry-go-round
first floor	second floor
cheerio	goodby